YOGA TEACHER

BY STEPHANIE FIN

T0014868

BLUE OWL
BOOKS

TIPS FOR CAREGIVERS

Social and emotional learning (SEL) helps children manage emotions, create and achieve goals, maintain relationships, learn how to feel empathy, and make good decisions. The SEL approach will help children establish positive habits in communication, cooperation, and decision-making. By incorporating SEL in early reading, children will be better equipped to build confidence and foster positive peer networks.

BEFORE READING

Talk to the reader about yoga.

Discuss: What did you know about yoga before reading this book? Have you tried yoga? If so, how did you feel after?

AFTER READING

Talk to the reader about how yoga can help us be mindful.

Discuss: How does yoga teach mindfulness? How can it help us focus? How can you add yoga to your daily routine?

SEL GOAL

Some students may struggle with self-management, making it hard to control impulses and sit still. Help readers build self-management skills by learning to stop, be present, and try yoga. How can they use mindful breathing to stay calm? Discuss how learning to do these things can help them regulate their thoughts and movements.

TABLE OF CONTENTS

CHAPTER 1

WHAT IS YOGA?

Eddie is distracted during class. He takes three deep breaths. This helps him be **mindful**. He learned this skill from his yoga teacher.

Yoga is an **ancient** practice. It comes from India. It involves mindfulness, breathing exercises, **meditation**, and movement. It helps people increase focus, build **confidence**, and develop **self-control**. It also helps people strengthen their bodies.

Yoga teachers are patient. Many may have found yoga helpful in their lives. They want to help others, too. They care for their students.

Teachers lead classes in many settings. Hospitals, yoga centers, community centers, and schools are some. When the weather is nice, some teachers lead classes outside!

A yoga teacher completes at least 200 hours of training in a special program.

Teachers **register** proof of their training. Most yoga centers require proof of registration to teach.

LEARNING MORE

Yoga teachers can get **certifications** by doing extra training. They can learn meditation. Or they may train to teach certain groups of people. Some train to teach children or people who are pregnant.

CHAPTER 2

HOW DO YOGA TEACHERS HELP?

Yoga teachers help people move their bodies. How? They create **routines**. Routines are different for each class. Some are more difficult than others.

Xander goes to yoga class after school. The teacher leads the class through a series of **poses**. The poses help Xander build strength, balance, and **flexibility**.

Some routines focus more on practicing mindfulness. Meditation is often part of yoga classes. It can help us tune in to our bodies. It can also help us focus and build memory skills. This can help us with other things, like taking a test or learning something new.

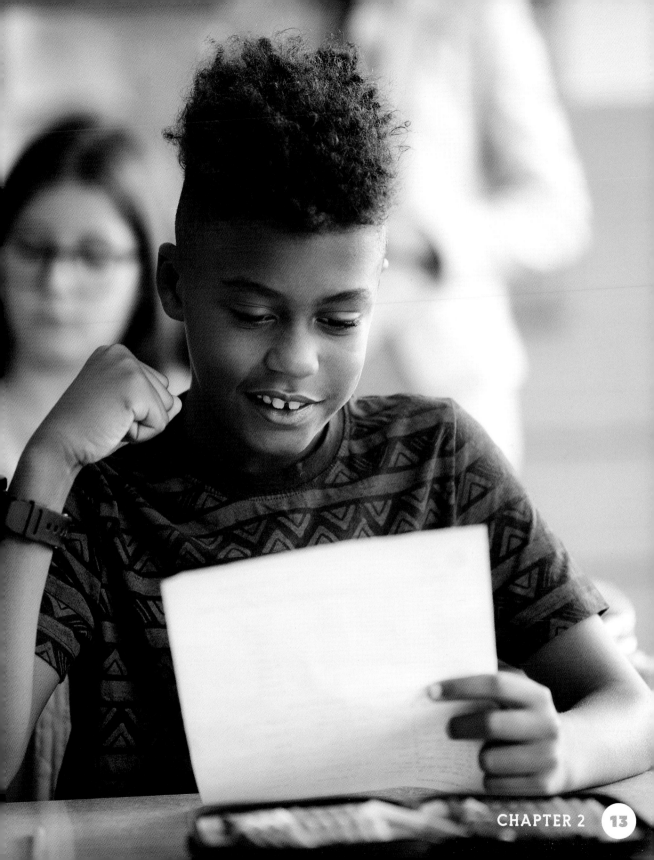

Alexis feels **anxious** about meeting new people at a friend's birthday party. Before she goes, she does a meditation her yoga teacher taught her. It helps her feel at ease. She is ready to have fun!

Elias is frustrated with his friend. He uses a deep breathing exercise his yoga teacher taught him. Now he feels less frustrated. He is better able to respond to **stress**.

WHERE CAN YOU DO YOGA?

You can practice yoga anywhere! Try a deep breathing exercise on the way to school. Strike a yoga pose while waiting in line. Meditate in bed to help you relax and sleep.

CHAPTER 3

WHO DO THEY HELP?

Yoga can help with many different things. Poses and mindful breathing help athletes focus. It can also help them build flexibility.

Yoga helps hospital patients deal with the stress of being ill. It helps them be calm and mindful.

Yoga classes also take place in classrooms, prisons, and yoga centers. Some teachers give private lessons.

Yoga teachers work hard to help others. They help people find inner peace.

MUSIC AND MEDITATION

Yoga routines don't have to be silent! They can be done with music. They usually end with a calming meditation.

GOALS AND TOOLS

GROW WITH GOALS

Yoga teachers must be able to connect with others. Try working on these goals.

Goal: Find one new person to talk to today. Ask that person questions about their life.

Goal: Name one emotion you felt today. Talk to a trusted adult or a friend about how you felt and why you felt that way.

Goal: Make a list of ways you can connect with friends, family, or classmates.

TRY THIS!

Try child's pose! This gentle stretch helps you connect to your breath and check in with your body. Place your hands and knees on the floor. Spread your knees wider than your shoulders but keep your big toes touching. Be mindful with your movements. Slowly, bring your forehead to rest on the floor. Relax your shoulders and jaw. Close your eyes. Take five slow, deep breaths. What do you notice?

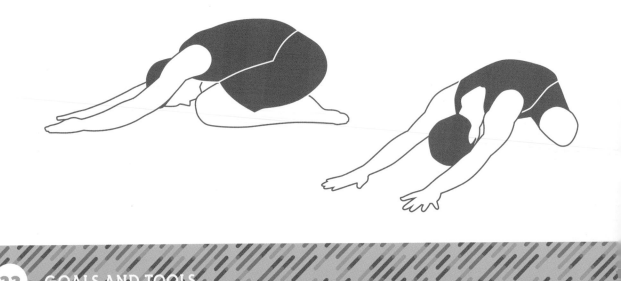

GLOSSARY

ancient
Belonging to a period long ago.

anxious
Worried or very eager to do something.

certifications
Statuses, specialties, or levels that someone has achieved as additional training.

confidence
A belief that you have the necessary ability to succeed.

flexibility
The ability to bend and move easily.

meditation
The act of thinking deeply and quietly.

mindful
Focused on the present moment and calmly recognizing and accepting your feelings, thoughts, and sensations.

poses
Positions or postures.

register
To get certified to do something.

routines
Practiced sequences of actions.

self-control
The ability to restrain or control oneself, especially relating to one's feelings and actions.

stress
Mental or emotional strain or pressure.

TO LEARN MORE

FACT SURFER

Finding more information is as easy as 1, 2, 3.

1. Go to www.factsurfer.com

2. Enter "**yogateacher**" into the search box.

3. Choose your book to see a list of websites.

INDEX

Blue Owl Books are published by Jump!, 5357 Penn Avenue South, Minneapolis, MN 55419, www.jumplibrary.com

Copyright © 2024 Jump! International copyright reserved in all countries. No part of this book may be reproduced in any form without written permission from the publisher.

Library of Congress Cataloging-in-Publication Data

Names: Finne, Stephanie, author.
Title: Yoga teacher / by Stephanie Finne.
Description: Minneapolis, MN: Jump!, Inc., [2024]
Series: SEL careers | Includes index.
Audience: Ages 7–10
Identifiers: LCCN 2023000290 (print)
LCCN 2023000291 (ebook)
ISBN 9798885246460 (hardcover)
ISBN 9798885246477 (paperback)
ISBN 9798885246484 (ebook)
Subjects: LCSH: Yoga–Juvenile literature. | Yoga–Study and teaching–Juvenile literature. | Yoga teachers–Juvenile literature. |
Yoga teachers–Vocational guidance–Juvenile literature.
Classification: LCC RA781.67 .F56 2024 (print)
LCC RA781.67 (ebook)
DDC 613.7/046023–dc23/eng/20230202
LC record available at https://lccn.loc.gov/2023000290
LC ebook record available at https://lccn.loc.gov/2023000291

Editor: Eliza Leahy
Designer: Molly Ballanger
Content Consultant: Laura Villano, RYT

Photo Credits: SDI Productions/iStock, cover; FatCamera/iStock, 1, 8–9, 11, 20–21; gresei/Shutterstock, 3; xavierarnau/iStock, 4; wavebreakmedia/Shutterstock, 5;
Kobus Louw/iStock, 6–7; May_Chanikran/Shutterstock, 10; Drazen Zigic/iStock, 12–13; aldomurillo/iStock, 14–15; Westend61/Getty, 16–17; Michael Zagaris/Oakland Athletics/
Getty, 18; Art_Photo/Shutterstock, 19.

Printed in the United States of America at Corporate Graphics in North Mankato, Minnesota.